Life Inside My Head

Beanie Bewell

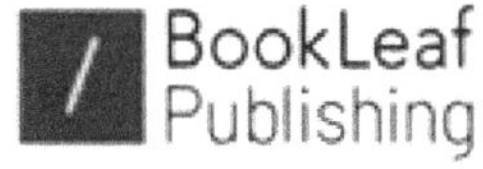

BookLeaf Publishing

Presentation by *BookLeaf Publishing*

Web: www.bookleafpub.com

E-mail: info@bookleafpub.com

ISBN: 9789357211376

First edition 2022

DEDICATION

To everyone who has had overwhelming big feelings they didn't know how to process. I see you, I hear you, I am you.

Rachel

My therapist said, "say more about your
feelings."
I told her I'm one minor inconvenience away
From losing my mind, just trying to survive.
I'm sick of saying goodbyes
Before I get to say hello.
To the little loves of my life
I didn't get to watch grow

I told her
I'm sick of being sad and feeling shitty
Too much caffeine, I'm always jittery
How did constant grief
Become a part of my story
How did I get stuck
In this grief purgatory

Celia

How do you say goodbye
to something you never got to hold?
How is it possible
to love something so much it hurts
without even knowing they exist?
Sweet child I didn't get to know.
You never got a chance to grow old.
Baby, you died before you were born.
I dream about what your life could have been.
Brown hair, doe eyes, long and lanky like your
daddy.
Your laugh my favorite melody.
You are a part of me,
marked on me, eternally.
Baby, it isn't fair
you were taken from me so damn early.
Sweet Celia Mae, this is me trying.
Hold on until you can see me,
and stay in the arms of Grace.

Hypeman

There are two kinds of people
Ones who bring color
And ones who take it
Ones who make your cheeks flush
And ones who drain it from your face
Ones who make you dress
like you should blend in and stay unnoticed
and ones who tell you to wear beautifully bright
colors
so more people see you
Ones who hide you and
Ones who brag about you

From Body to Mind

How many times
have I carried you
through the night
when you were tired on the floor
Ready to give up the fight
With tears in your eyes
And panic in your veins
Hands clenched tight
with half moon stains
When nothing feels the same
How many times have I kept you alive
When all you wanted was to die

Paxton

I hope when you think of yourself,
you are kinder than I have been
to myself.

I hope your heart swells with pride
when you think about everything
you've accomplished.

I hope you remember the days
you thought you wouldn't survive,
but did anyway.

I hope generations of silent trauma
ends with your voice,
clear and powerful.

I hope you know there are people
in your corner
who love you.

Love letter to a stranger

You may feel
like there is a world inside your head
that no one understands

You may feel
trapped by your indescribably big feelings
that hurt to express

You may feel
overwhelmed by bright lights and big crowds
unable to speak

You may feel
like you are too much and live
behind a mask

You may feel
imprisoned by your lonely thoughts
but I understand you.

Strong Feelings

Do my feelings make you uncomfortable?
When I feel things strongly, does it make you
want to run?
I saw the terror on your face you tried to hide
When I told you I wanted to die
I have strong feelings I keep to myself
Because I'm afraid of the effects on somebody
else
I have strong thoughts I continue to hide
Because I'd rather feel dread and want to die
Than see the panic in my sweet partner's eyes

Reality Check

There's a line in waitress that says,
"It's addictive the minute you let yourself think
The things that I say just might matter to
someone"
it was just another line
Until you told me
the night I picked you up
I saved your life.
That you had been researching
Painless ways to die
It was no longer a line in a song
But a reality
The things that I say matter
They mattered in the biggest
And most important way
I had something to do with keeping you alive
It's a beautiful thing sometimes
That words can be so powerful

Bear

I know I thank you all the time
For loving me
And if it's anything like how I love you
It's the easiest thing I do on a daily basis
But it means so much
To a girl who spent most of her life
Thinking she wasn't good enough
That she was unlovable
That she wasn't worth loving
I could thank you a thousand times
And it still wouldn't be good enough

Sweet Forgetfulness

For a brief moment
I forgot to be sad
For a brief moment
I didn't feel the bitterness
Sadness, and self loathing
I have been living in.

Fireflies

There are headlights
And there is darkness
And in between
There are fireflies
Hundreds of fireflies
And they are dancing
And sparkling down the long
Strips of endless highway
On a warm july night

Stephen

I played it off as my fault
It was what I wore
A black shirt and coffee bean shorts
Too provocative for a teenage boy
But not too provocative for work
It was how I acted
It was because my, "no" was too flirty
But it was a no just the same.
Consent once
Does not mean consent all the time.
Fuck you, Stephen

Jay

My friend
You should have your own
Page
Chapter
Book
In my life

Pride

If you accomplished something
that's been hard for you,
no matter how small,
I'm proud of you.

If you didn't get it done today,
I'm still proud of you.
Living is hard, and the fact that you're still here
is a testament to how strong you are.

Redolent

Your smell hit my brain
so crazy, amazing
my vision went hazy
the world went away
foggy and strange
I can hardly contain
my heart in my chest
like I'm being possessed
how could I forget
the things that you said
like, "I'll love you forever,"
when you just left

Double Standard

It's in the moments
Of unintentional vulnerability
When I catch glimpses
Of your brokenness
I feel safe
It's in other's vulnerability
I am secure
It's in my vulnerability
I am in danger
Your brokenness is beautiful
Mine is irreparable

Flannel

You wore my flannel for two hours
The first night we cooked together
It smells like
An evening in early fall
Spent laughing too loudly with strangers
And flying down hills
Pretending to be brave
It smells like
The first time you put your arms around me
And told me to trust you
It smells like
An all nighter spent driving through
Minneapolis
And watching 50 first dates in my car
It smells like
The way the sound of your laughter makes me
feel
Joyful, familiar, calming
It smells like
A January afternoon spent naked in my bed
While you whisper
"We'll never be closer than we are right now"
It smells like
Feelings I thought I had felt
Until I met you

In a Week

Monday:
I spent my day filled with giddy anxiety
I drank my first slushie of the week
They didn't have my favorite flavor
Tuesday:
the night we broke up i cried
And recklessly drove to campus
I stopped for my second slushie
The employees didn't charge me
Wednesday:
The day after we broke up, I spent the day
Wondering if you were okay
I couldn't handle thinking about you anymore
So i took a five hour nap and forgot to eat
Thursday:
Two days after we broke up
I tried to see my friends
Instead i fell asleep between them
My unconscious easier than thinking of you
Friday:
Three days after we broke up
I bought a cactus
I thought it might help
It didn't
Saturday:

Four days after we broke up
I spent the day with my roommate
Thinking thrift shopping would distract me
I couldn't stop wondering if you'd like my new
bikini
Sunday:
Five days after we broke up
My sister didn't believe i was eating
She sent me home with frozen chicken
I never ate it
Monday:
Six days after we broke up
I invited friends over to watch movies
I kissed my ex boyfriend on the balcony
Needing to feel loved
Tuesday:
Seven days after we broke up
I binge watched grey's anatomy
I packed to get away
And took your picture off my wall

Bear

I'm thankful for those
Who show up when I need them
I am thankful for those
Who show up before I even ask
You have always, always
Shown up for me

Cassidy Shay

I don't think
I could ever love
Anyone more
Than I love him
And yet
I seem to fall
In love with him
More every day

When I was 13
My body begged to be kissed
But when the bottle stopped
The boy said no way
Not her
That's gross

When I was 15,
A church boy grabbed my boobs
And held me tight
As I fought to push him away
My best friend got mad
Because she wanted him

When I was 18
A friend asked me to the park
When he pushed against me
I tried to pull away
And he held tighter
Touching other parts of me

When I was 22
A boy whispered sweet nothings
He got me into bed
Got what he wanted

And left

When I was 22
A boy showed up on my balcony
With a box of my favorite things
And tried to leave
So I'd know he didn't expect anything

When I was 22
the same boy showed up
just because he knew I was sad
And walked with me till 1 am

When I was 22
The boy made me
Fall in love
So deeply
And fully